The Amistad: The Slave Revolt and Legal Case that Changed the World

By Charles River Editors

A 19th century painting depicting the Amistad

About Charles River Editors

Charles River Editors provides superior editing and original writing services across the digital publishing industry, with the expertise to create digital content for publishers across a vast range of subject matter. In addition to providing original digital content for third party publishers, we also republish civilization's greatest literary works, bringing them to new generations of readers via ebooks.

Sign up here to receive updates about free books as we publish them, and visit Our Kindle Author Page to browse today's free promotions and our most recently published Kindle titles.

Introduction

A 19th century engraving depicting the revolt on the Amistad

The Amistad

"25,000 slaves were brought into Cuba every year – with the wrongful compliance of, and personal profit by, Spanish officials." – Dr. Richard Madden

"Now, the unfortunate Africans whose case is the subject of the present representation, have been thrown by accidental circumstances into the hands of the authorities of the United States Government whether these persons shall recover the freedom to which they are entitled, or whether they shall be reduced to slavery, in violation of known laws and contracts publicly passed, prohibiting the continuance of the African slave-trade by Spanish subjects." – Henry Stephen Fox, British diplomat

By the early 19th century, several European nations had banned slavery, but while the United States had banned the international slave trade, slavery was still legal in the country itself. As a result, there was still a strong financial motive for merchants and slave traders to attempt to bring slaves to the Western hemisphere, and a lot of profits to be gained from successfully sneaking slaves into the American South and the Caribbean by way of locations like Havana, Cuba.

At the same time, the cruelties of the slave trade often led to desperate attempts by slaves or would-be slaves to avoid the horrific fate that they were either experiencing or about to face. In 1831, Nat Turner's revolt shocked the South and scared plantation owners across the country, while also bringing the issue of slavery to the forefront of the national debate. But just years after Turner's rebellion was quickly put down, the United States was embroiled in another similar controversy as a result of the successful insurrection aboard the *Amistad*, a Spanish schooner that was carrying Africans taken from modern day Sierra Leone and brought across the Atlantic to Cuba.

In 1839, the *Amistad* was loaded in Havana with Africans who had been brought across the ocean to be made slaves, but after the ship left Havana for another location on Cuba, the Africans escaped their shackles, killed the captain, and took over the ship. When they demanded to be taken back to Africa, the ship's crew instead sailed north, and the ship was ultimately captured off the coast of Long Island in New York by the USS *Washington*. All of this resulted in one of the most famous maritime cases in history, and one that affected not just the international slave trade ban but also how jurisdiction over such a case was determined. While the British were interested in enforcing the ban on the slave trade, Spain wanted to protect its own rights by asserting that their property (crew and ship) could not be subjected to American jurisdiction, and that since slavery was legal in Cuba, a foreign country had no right to determine the legal status of the Africans aboard the *Amistad*. On top of that, both the Spanish slave traders intending to sail the ship around Cuba and the American captain who seized the *Amistad* claimed ownership of the Africans.

The legal case proceeded all the way up to the United States Supreme Court, which eventually affirmed a lower court ruling that allowed the Africans to be returned home as free men, but not before the British and Spanish used diplomatic and political leverage to try to influence the outcome. Ultimately, the rebellion on the *Amistad* and the case that followed became a watershed moment in the debate over slavery and abolition in America about 20 years before the Civil War.

The Amistad: The Slave Revolt and Legal Case that Changed The World chronicles the events that led up to one of history's most famous slave uprisings, and the lasting legacy of the case that determined the fate of the Africans on the ship. Along with pictures of important people, places, and events, you will learn about the *Amistad* like never before, in no time at all.

The Amistad: The Slave Revolt and Legal Case that Changed the World
About Charles River Editors
Introduction
   Chapter 1: The Amistad's Journey
   Chapter 2: Under What Authority
   Chapter 3: Mutiny and Murder?
   Chapter 4: Unfortunate Under Such Circumstances
   Chapter 5: Supreme Arguments
   Chapter 6: The Ruling
   Bibliography

Chapter 1: The Amistad's Journey

"The Africans of the Amistad were cast upon our coast in a condition perhaps as calamitous as could befall human beings, not by their own will - not with any intention hostile or predatory on their part, not even by the act of God as in the case of shipwreck, but by their own ignorance of navigation and the deception of one of their oppressors whom they had overpowered, and whose life they had spared to enable them by his knowledge of navigation to reach their native land. They were victims of the African slave trade, recently imported into the island of Cuba, in gross violation of the laws of the Island and of Spain; and by acts which our own laws have made piracy - punishable with death. They had indicated their natural right to liberty, by conspiracy, insurrection, homicide and capture and they were accused by the two Cuban Spaniards embarked with them in the ship, of murder and piracy - and they were claimed by the same two Cuban Spaniards, accessories after the fact to the slave-trade piracy, by which they had been brought from Africa to Cuba, as their property, because they had bought them from slave-trade pirates." John Quincy Adams in a letter written in November 1839

The legend of the *Amistad* began in June 1839, when a group of young men were captured illegally in Africa and were set to be transported against their will to Havana, Cuba. Given the ban on the slave trade, the completely illegal nature of their capture would prove to be an integral part of the court case that would make them, and their captors, famous. Congressman Joshua Reed Giddings, an ardent abolitionist, spelled out some of the background in the trial that followed: "[A]s early as 1817 Spain took upon herself the most solemn obligations to abolish this slave trade…In perfect good faith, the Crown of Spain, by its decadal order, issued soon after, declared the slave trade abolished throughout her dominions, including her colonial possessions; and asserted the freedom of all Africans who should be thereafter imported into any of her national or colonial ports…[C]ertain Cuban slave dealers continued to violate the laws and treaties of their own Government, the rights of human nature, and the laws of God, by importing and enslaving the unoffending people of Africa. In 1839 they imported a cargo of these inoffensive victims to Havana, in the Island of Cuba…[T]hey were seized in Africa about the middle of April 1839, force carried on board the slave ship, and on the 12th June of that year they were landed in Havana, and imprisoned in the barracoons of that city."

Giddings

Shortly after the Africans landed in Havana, they were purchased by two Spanish citizens, Jose Ruiz and Pedro Montes, who planned to sell the slaves to plantation owners elsewhere on the island. As a result, a ship called *La Amistad* ("The Friendship") left Havana to travel to the province of Puerto Principe, also located on the island of Cuba. At that time, Cuba was still a Spanish colony.

A replica of the *Amistad* is now docked at Mystic Seaport, Connecticut, home of the largest maritime museum in the world.

The ship was under the command of Captain Ramón Ferrer, with Ruiz and Montes serving as crew and a cook onboard. The ship's "cargo" consisted of 53 Africans being sent by the governor-general of Cuba to Puerto Principe, but there was a problem with his plan for them. As Giddings later explained, "These Africans were in no way parties to these permits, knew nothing of their being granted; and I need say their rights could not be affected in any way by them…they were in no respect admissible evidence against the Negroes, who had been imported in fraud, and in violation of Spanish treaties and Spanish laws."

More problems arose when the crew ran out of food and water five days into what was supposed to be a four-day voyage. Naturally, the ship's crew decided to keep what little provisions that were left for themselves, leaving the poor Africans to starve. Some of the Africans would later claim that the cook, a man named Celestino, admitted to them that the crew might eventually resort to killing the Africans themselves for food.

Ultimately, the captives decided to take their chances with a mutiny and to die as free men rather than live as slaves. Thus, as Giddings continued, "On the 1st day of July, while sailing along the eastern coast of the Island, the Africans rose and claimed their freedom. The captain and cook attempted to reduce them to subjection, and were slain; Montes and Ruiz, and the two sailors, surrendered the ship [to the] Africans. They immediately sent the sailors to shore in the boat, and retaining Montes and Ruiz on board, directed them to steer the ship for Africa. But, during the darkness of the night, they directed their course northwardly, and on the 26th of August, being sixty days from the time of leaving Havana, they came to anchor off the Connecticut coast, near the eastern shore of Long Island. While the vessel was thus riding at anchor, Lieutenant Gedney, of the ship Washington, engaged in the coast survey of the United States, took possession of her, and of the cargo and people on board, and carried them into the port of New London."

The leader of the mutineers was a young man, Sengbe Pieh, who later became known as Joseph Cinqué. Cinqué was able to escape his own bonds by using a file that had been given to him by a woman during their trip from Africa to Cuba, and he then freed the other captives. In addition to the captain and the cook, two of the Africans lost their lives during the skirmish.

1840 portrait of Cinqué

A sketch depicting Cinqué in traditional Muslim garb

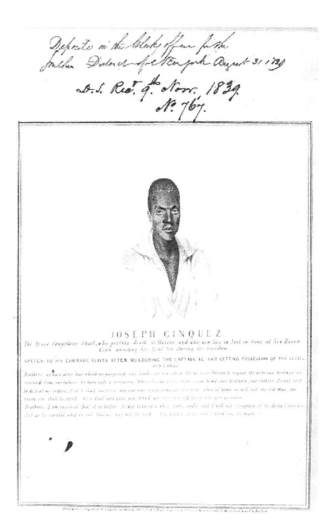

A depiction of Cinqué that appeared in a New York newspaper, *The Sun*, in August 1839

Thus, even though the Africans had successfully overrun the crew, their lack of nautical knowledge allowed the ship to be captured when it arrived at Culloden Point on Long Island on August 26, 1839. There was some misunderstanding as to when exactly the ship arrived in New York, with some records indicating that it was not until August 1840, but it's doubtful that the ship was at sea for over a year traveling from Cuba to New York. Furthermore, the *New London Gazette* reported the *Amistad*'s story on August 26, 1839, and in doing so, the paper presented a clearly biased account of how the ship arrived there:

> "While this vessel was sounding this day between Gardner's and Montauk Points, a schooner was seen lying in shore off Culloden Point, under circumstances so

suspicious as to authorize Lt. Com. Gedney to stand in to see what was her character--seeing a number of people on the beach with carts and horses, and a boat passing to and fro a boat was armed and dispached with an officer to board her. On coming along side a number of negroes were discovered on her deck, and twenty or thirty more were on the beach--two white men came forward and claimed the protection of the officer. The schooner proved to be the "Amistad," Capt. Ramonflues, from the Havana bound to Guanaja, Port Principe, with 54 blacks and two passengers on board

    The situation of the two whites was all this time truly deplorable, being treated with the greatest severity, and Pedro Montes, who had charge of the navigation, was suffering from two severe wounds, one in the head and one in the arm, their lives threatened every instant. He was ordered to change the course again for the coast of Africa, the negroes themselves steering by the sun in the day time, while at night he would alter their course so as to bring them back to their original place of destination.--They remained three days off Long Island, to the Eastward of Providence, after which time they were two months on the ocean, sometimes steering to the Eastward, and whenever an occasson [sic] would permit the whites would alter the course to the Northward and Westward, always in hopes of falling in with some vessel of war, or being enabled to run into some port, when they would be relieved from their horrid situation.

    Several times they were boarded by vessels; once by an American schooner from Kingston. On these occasions the whites were ordered below, while the negroes communicated and traded with the vessel; the schooner from Kingston supplied them with a demijohn of water, for the moderate sum of one doubloon--this schooner, whose name was not ascertained, finding that the negroes had plenty of money, remained lashed alongside the "Amistad" for twenty-four hours, though they must have been aware that all was not right on board, and probably suspected the character of the vessel--that was on the 18th of the present month; the vessel was steered to the northward and westward, and on the 20th instant, distant from N.Y. 25 miles, the pilot boat No. 3 came alongside and gave the negroes some apples. She was also hailed by No. 4; when the latter boat came near, the negroes armed themselves and would not permit her to board them; they were so exasperated with the two whites for bringing them so much out of their way that they expected every moment to be murdered."

    When some of the men left the ship to go ashore for food and water, the USS *Washington* spotted the ship, which they had been told was stolen. Lieutenant Thomas R. Gedney, then in command of the *Washington*, captured the ship and those aboard, and he subsequently sailed the ship to New London, Connecticut, where slavery was legal.

People in town quickly heard of the ship's arrival and the story of what supposedly happened aboard it, all of which made good grist for sensationalist accounts. A reporter sent to investigate later wrote, "On board the brig we also saw Cinqué, the master spirit and hero of this bloody tragedy, in irons. He is about five feet eight inches in height, 25 or 26 years of age, of erect figure, well built, and very active. He is said to be a match for any two men aboard the schooner. His countenance, for a native African, is unusually intelligent, evincing uncommon decision and coolness, with a composure characteristic of true courage, and nothing to mark him a malicious man. ... On her deck were grouped amid various goods and arms, the remnant of her Ethiopian crew, some decked in the most fantastic manner, in silks and finery, pilfered from the cargo, while others, in a state of nudity, emaciated to mere skeletons, lay coiled upon the decks. ... On the forward hatch we unconsciously rested our hand on a cold object, which we soon discovered to be a naked corpse, enveloped in a pall of black bombazine. On removing its folds, we beheld the rigid countenance and glazed eye of a poor Negro who died last night. His mouth was unclosed and still wore the ghastly expression of his last struggle."

A contemporary portrait of one of the Africans on the *Amistad*

Chapter 2: Under What Authority

"I do not, in fact, understand how a foreign court of justice can be considered competent to take cognizance of an offence committed on board of a Spanish vessel, by Spanish subjects, and against Spanish subjects, in the waters of a Spanish territory; for it was committed on the coasts of this island, and under the flag of this nation." - Cavallero Pedro Alcantara Argaiz, Spanish minister

The matter first came before the courts when Montes and Ruiz tried to claim ownership of the Africans. According to court transcripts, "On the 29th of August, 1839 — being precisely two months and one day from the time of leaving the port of Havana — Montes and Ruiz filed their claim in the district court of the United States, demanding these Africans as their slaves. On the 19th September, 1839, the Africans filed their answers to claim of Montes and Ruiz ... denying that they were, or ever had been, slaves to Montes and Ruiz, or to any other person; but that they were, and ever had been, free."

Making the matter even more complex, Montes and Ruiz were not the only ones who felt that they had a right to claim ownership of the "cargo," because Gedney also claimed ownership based on the laws of salvage. Connecticut Judge James Dixon explained, "The vessel, with the Negroes on board, having been brought by Lieutenant Gedney into the district of Connecticut, was there, by him, libeled for salvage in the district court of the United States. A libel for salvage was also filed by other parties, who claimed to have aided in saving the ship by arresting the Negroes on shore."

Furthermore, the others mentioned as claiming rights to the Africans included "Henry Green and Pelatiah Fordham and others, [who] filed a petition and answer to the libel, claiming salvage out of the property proceeded against by Thomas R. Gedney and others, and stating, that before the *Amistad* was seen or boarded by the officers and crew of the Washington, they had secured a portion of the Negroes who had come on shore, and had thus aided in saving the vessel and cargo." Even the Spanish government became involved when "[o]n the 19th of September, the district attorney of the United States for the district of Connecticut filed an information, or libel, setting forth the claim of the Spanish Government under the treaty of 1795, renewed in 1821."

Up to this point, the case was not that unique, as maritime cases related to salvage came through the courts on a regular basis during the 19th century. However, the new wrinkle appeared when the Africans, with the help of several sympathetic American attorneys, filed a claim to their own freedom: "To these various libels, the Negroes, Cinqué and others ... on the 7th of January, 1840, filed an answer, denying that they were slaves or the property of Ruiz and Montes, or that the court could ... exercise any jurisdiction over their persons, by reason of the premises; and praying that they might be dismissed. They specially set forth and insisted, that they were native-born Africans; that they were born free, and still of right ought to be free, and not slaves; that they were, on or about the 15th day of April, 1839, unlawfully kidnapped and forcibly and wrongfully carried on board a certain vessel, on the coast of Africa, which was unlawfully engaged in the slave trade, and were unlawfully transported in the same vessel to the

Island of Cuba, for the purpose of being unlawfully sold as slaves; that Ruiz and Montes … made a pretended purchase of them, that afterwards … caused them, without law or right, to be placed on board the said *Amistad*, to be transported to some place unknown to them, to be enslaved for life; that on the voyage they rose and took possession of the vessel, intending to return therewith to their native country, or to seek an asylum in some free State."

Of course, the Africans were at a distinct disadvantage when it came to defending themselves against this action, which Giddings later pointed out: "Here I will remark that the Africans were strangers in a strange land, ignorant of any language save their native dialect — without friends, without influence, and without money. One would have reasonably supposed that the sympathies of all men and all Government officers would have been enlisted in favor of these persecuted exiles, who had been thus torn from their homes, their country, their kindred and friends. The dictates of our nature are in favor of the oppressed, the friendless, of those who are incapable of defending their own rights." However, as the case became public and federal leaders became involved, Giddings ruefully noted, "Yet I feel humbled, as an American, when I say that the President [Martin Van Buren] sent orders to the United States Attorney for the district of Connecticut, directing him to appear before the court, and in the name of the Spanish Minister to demand these Africans, in order that they may be delivered over to their pretended owners." Of course, Van Buren, who was seeking reelection in 1840, was much more concerned about the Southern slave owners whose votes he needed than appeasing the Spanish, but it did throw another angle into the already complicated case.

Van Buren

Chapter 3: Mutiny and Murder?

A page from a deposition in the mutiny case against the Africans

"Great Britain is also bound to remember that the law of Spain, which finally prohibited the slave-trade throughout the Spanish dominions, from the date of the 30th of May, 1820, the provisions of which law are contained in the King of Spain's royal cedula of the 19th December, was passed, in compliance with a treaty obligation to that effect, by which the Crown of Spain had bound itself to the Crown of Great Britain, and for which a valuable compensation, in return, was given by Great Britain to Spain; as may be seen by reference to the 2d, 3d, and 4th articles of a public treaty concluded between Great Britain and Spain on the 23d of September, 1817." – Henry Stephen Fox, British diplomat

Even as the civil case was ongoing to determine who if anyone owned the Africans, a case charging them with mutiny and murder commenced, and the first hearing was held aboard the *Washington* while most of the Africans were confined in a jail in New Haven, Connecticut. Beginning on August 29, Judge Andrew T. Judson heard charges and testimony concerning the 39 Africans accused of murdering the captain and the cook. During the trial, Ruiz testified, "I took an oar and tried to quell the mutiny. I cried 'No! No!' I then heard one of the crew cry murder. I then heard the captain order the cabin boy to go below and get some bread to throw among the Negroes, hoping to pacify them. I did not see the captain killed." Next, Montes added his testimony, saying that on the fourth night that the ship was out to sea, "[b]etween three and four [I] was awakened by a noise which was caused by blows to the mulatto cook. I went on deck and they attacked me. I seized a stick and a knife with a view to defend myself...At this time [Cinqué] wounded me on the head severely with one of the sugar knives, also on the arm. I then ran below and stowed myself between two barrels, wrapped up in a sail. [Cinqué] rushed after me and attempted to kill me, but was prevented by the interference of another man...I was then taken on deck and tied to the hand of Ruiz."

Following this hearing, Judson bound the case over to trial in a Connecticut circuit court, a federal court. Meanwhile, the Africans remained in custody, though they were apparently well treated and allowed a great deal of freedom to move about and be comfortable. The jailors seemed to have taken a liking to the children in the group and occasionally arranged for them to take rides in a wagon around the grounds. During this time, the Africans became a source of public curiosity and were seen by many in a very sympathetic light.

Perhaps concerned about the sympathy the Africans were receiving, Ruiz and Montes decided to go to work on public opinion. On the afternoon of the hearing, the following appeared in the New London newspaper: "The subscribers, Don Jose Ruiz, and Don Pedro Montes, in gratitude for their most unhoped for and providential rescue from the bands of a ruthless gang of African buccaneers and an awful death, would take the means of expressing, in some slight decree, their thankfulness and obligation to Lieut. Com T. R. Gedney, and the officers and crew of the U. S surveying brig Washington, for their decision in seizing the *Amistad*, and their unremitting kindness and hospitality in providing for their comfort on board their vessel, as well as the means they have taken for the protection of their property. We also must express our indebtedness to that nation whose flag they so worthily bear, with an assurance that the act will be duly appreciated by our most gracious sovereign, her Majesty the Queen of Spain."

Meanwhile, an abolitionist named Lewis Tappan banded with some of his fellow abolitionists to create the Friend of Amistad Africans Committee, and he then traveled to New Haven to meet the men he hoped to befriend in person. It was there he learned that the Africans were from the Mende tribe in Africa, and with that knowledge, he was able to secure a translator who would allow him to communicate with them. Tappan wrote, "I arrived here last Friday evening, with three men who are natives of Africa…to act as interpreters in conversing with Joseph Cinqué and his comrades. … You may imagine the joy manifested by these poor Africans, when they heard one of their own color address them in a friendly manner, and in a language they could comprehend! … I have read an ingenious and well written article in the Evening Post signed Veto, in which the learned writer presents a pretty full examination of the case of the schooner *Amistad*… [W]here there exists no treaty stipulation, as there does not at present between the United States and Spain…this country ought not to surrender persons situated as are Joseph Cinqué and his unfortunate countrymen, who are, by the act of God, thrown upon these shores to find, I trust, that protection and relief of which they had been, probably, forever deprived had it not been for this remarkable and providential interposition."

Lewis Tappan

The Africans may have gained a measure of relief from meeting Tappan and an interpreter, but their fates very much hung in the balance, and on September 6, Calderon de la Barca wrote to the American Secretary of State, John Forsyth, on behalf of the Spanish government. De la Barca made the following demands:

> "1st. That the vessel be immediately delivered up to her owner, together with every article found on board at the time of her capture by the Washington, without

any payment being exacted on the score of salvage, nor any charges made, other than those specified in the treaty of 1795, article 1st.

2d. That it be declared that no tribunal in the United States has the right to institute proceedings against, or to impose penalties upon, the subjects of Spain, for crimes committed on board a Spanish vessel, and in the waters of the Spanish territory.

3d. That the Negroes be conveyed to Havana, or be placed at the disposal of the proper authorities in that part of Her Majesty's dominions, in order to their being tried by the Spanish laws which they have violated; and that, in the meantime, they be kept in safe custody, in order to prevent their evasion.

4th. That if, in consequence of the intervention of the authorities of Connecticut, there should be any delay in the desired delivery of the vessel and the slaves, the owners both of the latter and of the former be indemnified for the injury that may accrue to them."

De la Barca then added, for good measure, what might be construed as a veiled threat: "In support of these claims, the undersigned invokes the law of nations, the stipulations of existing treaties, and those good feelings so necessary to the maintenance of the friendly relations that subsist between the two countries, and are so interesting to both".

Secretary of State Forsyth

The following week, on September 14, 1839, U.S. Supreme Court Justice Smith Thompson, who had convened the lower circuit court, heard requests from a federal attorney requesting that the Africans be turned over to President Van Buren for return to Cuba. Thompson decided that since the mutiny took place in international waters, American courts had no jurisdiction over the charges against the Africans. However, Thompson sent the civil case to the U.S. District Court for the District Court of Connecticut to decide who had ownership of the Africans on the *Amistad*.

Smith Thompson

In October 1839, with the help of Tappan and other members of the Friends committee, Cinqué and the other Africans filed charges against Ruiz and Montes for assault and false imprisonment. The two were arrested, and Montes quickly decided that he no longer had any interest in his "property," so he posted bail and boarded the first ship he could back to Cuba. Ruiz, on the other hand, found American jail enough to his liking that he decided to remain in the United States and stand trial. However, this situation did not last for long, as he too soon posted bail and returned to Cuba. As Iyunolu Folayan Osagie, author of *The Amistad Revolt: Memory, Slavery, and the Politics of Identity in the United States and Sierra Leone*, put it, Ruiz was "more comfortable in a New England setting (and entitled to many amenities not available to the Africans), [and] hoped to garner further public support by staying in jail...Ruiz, however, soon tired of his martyred lifestyle in jail and posted bond. Like Montez, he returned to Cuba".

Montes and Ruiz may have decided the trouble wasn't worth pursuing a case, but the Spanish government was furious that their citizens had been arrested in the first place. The Spanish ambassador, Cavallero Pedro Alcantara Argaiz, took a personal interest in the situation and demanded that the entire case related to the *Amistad* be thrown out of court. Furthermore, he insisted that the bail money the men posted be returned to them since "by the treaty of 1795, no obstacle or impediment" should have kept them from leaving.

However, the fact that Montes and Ruiz were indeed allowed to leave the United States was later used by the Africans' attorneys in their argument on behalf of the Africans' freedom: "Now, sir, when the *Amistad* came within our jurisdiction, when our laws spread their aegis over the people on board, it was a matter of course that those people were as free to go where they pleased, as were Montes and Ruiz. Indeed, those Spaniards were themselves restored to liberty by the force of our laws; and the Negroes, had they been held as legal slaves in Cuba, under Spanish laws, would have been as free, the moment they came within our jurisdiction, as were Montes and Ruiz."

Chapter 4: Unfortunate Under Such Circumstances

The wheels of justice slowed with the coming of winter; in November, the U.S. District Court for the District of Connecticut met to review the case but then chose to postpone trying it. Thus, they did not get around to hearing evidence until January 8, 1840, when the civil trial began in New Haven. The abolitionists spoke first, putting forth the argument that since Spain had made it illegal to capture and transport slaves to the United States in 1817, the Africans could not be legally owned by anyone but instead had been kidnapped. Therefore, they should be allowed to return to Africa. They also accused the Cuban government, and by extension the government of Spain, of falsifying documents to make it appear that the Africans in question had actually been born on the island.

On January 10, an American attorney, W. S. Holabird, countered the abolitionists' assertions while appearing in court on behalf of Spain's attorney (A.G. Vega). Holabird asserted, "That [Vega] is a Spanish subject; that he resided in the island of Cuba several years; that he knows the laws of that island on the subject of slavery; that there was no law that was considered in force in the island of Cuba, that prohibited the bringing in African slaves; that the court of mixed commissioners had no jurisdiction, except in cases of capture on the sea; that newly-imported African Negroes were constantly brought to the island, and after landing, were bon a fide transferred from one owner to another, without any interference by the local authorities or the mixed commission, and were held by the owners, and recognized as lawful property; that slavery was recognized in Cuba, by all the laws that were considered in force there; that the native language of the slaves was kept up on some plantations, for years. That the barracoons are public markets, where all descriptions of slaves are sold and bought; that the papers of the *Amistad* are genuine, and are in the usual form; that it was not necessary to practice any fraud, to obtain such papers from the proper officers of the government…"

On January 15, Judge Andrew Judson, on behalf of the court, ruled in favor of the Africans and ordered the President of the United States to return them to their homeland. However, Van Buren refused to carry out the court's order and instead instructed Holabird to file an appeal with the U.S. Circuit Court for the Connecticut District. The notion that the American president was not just advocating Spanish interests but actually directing Spain's legal course of action appalled many citizens in and around Connecticut and led the editor of the *Hartford Courant* to publish the following scathing editorial on February 10, 1840: "We are informed Martin Van Buren addressed a letter to the Judge recommending and urging him to order the Africans to be taken back to Havana in a government vessel, to be sold there as slaves…The letter of the President, recommending that these poor unfortunate Africans be sent into perpetual bondage, is said to contain statements disgraceful to the high station of its author, and which, were they published, would excite the indignation of every Republican freeman in the land. What will the friends of liberty say to this? Surely Martin Van Buren is playing the part of a tyrant with a high hand - else why this tampering with our courts of justice, this Executive usurpation, and this heartless violation of the inalienable rights of man? Of the truth of the above there is no doubt, and we leave the unprincipled author of such a proceeding in the hands of a just and high-minded People."

In April 1840, the United States Senate also weighed in on the case. Under the leadership of Southern statesman John C. Calhoun, the members voted to issue two resolutions that they hoped might guide the courts:

> "1. Resolved—That a ship or vessel on the high seas, in time of peace, engaged in a lawful voyage, is according to the laws of nations under the exclusive jurisdiction of the state to which her flag belongs as much as if constituting a part of its own domain.
>
> 2. Resolved—That if such ship or vessel should be forced, by stress of weather, or other unavoidable cause into the port, and under the jurisdiction of a friendly power, she and her cargo, and persons on board, with their property, and all the rights belonging to their personal relations, as established by the laws of the state to which they belong, would be placed under the protection which the laws of nations extend to the unfortunate under such circumstances."

Ironically, these resolutions were later cited not by those working against the Africans' freedom but by those in favor of it.

Chapter 5: Supreme Arguments

"This review of all the proceedings of the Executive I have made with utmost pain, because it was necessary to bring it fully before your Honors, to show that the course of that department had been dictated, throughout, not by justice but by sympathy – and a sympathy the most partial and injust. And this sympathy prevailed to such a degree, among all the persons concerned in this business, as to have perverted their minds with regard to all the most sacred principles of law and right, on which the liberties of the United States are founded; and a course was pursued, from the beginning to the end, which was not only an outrage upon the persons whose lives and liberties were at stake, but hostile to the power and independence of the judiciary itself." – John Quincy Adams

In August 1840, the African prisoners were transferred from cells in New Haven to Westville, a New Haven suburb, where they received an esteemed visitor: Congressman John Quincy Adams, son of the second president of the United States and a former president in his own right. Of all the causes that Quincy Adams championed during the final years of his life, none was as dear to his heart as ending slavery. In fact, in order to bring the issue into public debate, he brought to the floor of the United States House of Representatives a petition for the New England states to secede from the Union if the institution of slavery remained legal. Though he claimed his petition was merely meant to get the debate rolling, his fellow Congressmen were enraged by his actions.

In response to his action, his political opponents called for his censure, and he was tried for two long weeks. Unconcerned about a possible conviction, he used the debates not to defend himself but to castigate slave owners and their representatives in Congress, singling out future presidential candidate Stephen Douglas for his particular ire. He also scolded Congress for the "gag rule" that kept the debate over slavery from being addressed directly in Congressional debates. While the rule remained unchanged, so did Quincy Adams. In 1838, he wrote to a friend, "The conflict between the principle of liberty and the fact of slavery is coming gradually to an issue. Slavery has now the power, and falls into convulsions at the approach of freedom. That the fall of slavery is predetermined in the counsels of Omnipotence I cannot doubt; it is a part of the great moral improvement in the condition of man, attested by all the records of history. But the conflict will be terrible, and the progress of improvement perhaps retrograde before its final progress to consummation."

John Quincy Adams

After Quincy Adams visited the men, he offered to represent them before the U.S. Circuit Court of the Connecticut District, and due in part to his excellent arguments, the U.S. Circuit Court upheld the District Court's decision in September 1840.

Still unwilling to give up, Van Buren ordered the case appealed to the United States Supreme Court, and that court opened its session on February 23, 1841 with oral arguments from Attorney General Henry D. Gilpin. Gilpin was a Van Buren appointee and owed his career to the goodwill of the president, so he was fully committed to winning the case.

In the argument, Gilpin stated:

> "[T]he minister of Spain demands that the vessel, cargo, and Negroes, be restored, pursuant to the 9th article of the treaty of 27th October, 1795, which provides that 'all ships and merchandise of what nature whatsoever, which shall be rescued out of the hands of any pirates or robbers, on the high seas, shall be brought into some port of either state, and shall be delivered into the custody of the officers of that port, in order to be taken care of and restored entire to the true proprietor, as soon as due and sufficient proof shall be made concerning the property thereof.'

The only inquiries, then, that present themselves, are,

1. Has 'due and sufficient proof concerning the property thereof' been made?

2. If so, have the United States a right to interpose in the manner they have done, to obtain its restoration to the Spanish owners?

If these inquiries result in the affirmative, then the decree of the Circuit Court was erroneous, and ought to be reversed."

In answering the questions he had just posed, Gilpin set forth a number of arguments:

"It is submitted that there has been due and sufficient proof concerning the property to authorize its restoration.

It is not denied that, under the laws of Spain, Negroes may be held as slaves, … nor will it be denied, if duly proved to be such, they are subject to restoration as much as other property, when coming under the provisions of this treaty. Now these Negroes are declared, by the certificates of the Governor General, to be slaves, and the property of the Spanish subjects … the highest functionary of the government in Cuba; his public acts are the highest evidence of any facts stated by him, within the scope of his authority. It is within the scope of his authority to declare what is property, and what are the rights of the subjects of Spain, within his jurisdiction, in regard to property.

Now, in the intercourse of nations, there is no rule better established than this: that full faith is to be given to such acts -- to the authentic evidence of such acts. The question is not whether the act is right or wrong; it is, whether the scope of what had been done, and whether it is an act within the scope of the authority. We are to inquire only whether the power existed, and whether it was exercised, and how it was exercised; not whether it was rightly or wrongly exercised."

The glaring hole in Gilpin's argument was that significant evidence indicated that the Governor General of Cuba was wrong (either knowingly or unknowingly) about the validity of the Africans' slavery. Knowing that he could not effectively defend against this evidence, Gilpin declared the right of the governor not to be questioned: "Where property on board of a vessel is brought into a foreign port, the documentary evidence, whether it be a judicial decree, or the ship's papers, accompanied by possession, is the best evidence of ownership, and that to which Courts of justice invariably look." He further added, "But it is said that this evidence is insufficient, because it is in point of fact fraudulent and untrue. The ground of this assertion is, that the slaves were not property in Cuba, at the date of the document signed by the Governor General; because they had been lately introduced into that island from Africa, and persons so introduced were free. To this it is answered that, if it were so, this Court will not look beyond the authentic evidence under the official certificate of the Governor General; that, if it would, there is not such evidence as this Court can regard to be sufficient to overthrow the positive statement of that document; and that, if the evidence were even deemed sufficient to show the recent introduction of the Negroes, it does not establish that they were free at the date of the certificate."

Gilpin knew that he would get the court's attention with this argument, for if the United States felt that it could seize property from another country just because that property was on a ship within their waters, it would be tantamount to condoning piracy. The same was true if it declared papers recognized as valid by another country invalid in America. The biggest threat, of course, was that other countries could retaliate by saying the same thing about American papers. Gilpin continued, "Would this Court be justified, on evidence such as this, in setting aside the admitted certificate of the Governor General? Would such evidence, in one of our own Courts, be deemed adequate to set aside a judicial proceeding, or an act of a public functionary, done in the due exercise of his office? How, then, can it be adequate to such an end, before the tribunals of a foreign country, when they pass upon the internal municipal acts of another government; and when the endeavor is made to set them aside, in a matter relating to their own property and people?"

Of course, Gilpin knew that no matter how he might like to phrase it, there was a bigger, more morally and politically charged issue involved in the case. In fact, it was the very issue that would make the case itself one of the most famous maritime cases in history. As he stated the question, "[I]is there any difference between property in slaves and other property? They existed as property at the time of the treaty in perhaps every nation of the globe; they still exist as property in Spain and the United States; they can be demanded as property in the states of this Union to which they fly, and where by the laws they would not, if domiciled, be property. If, then, they are property, the rules laid down in regard to property extend to them. If they are found on board of a vessel, the evidence of property should be that which is recognized as the best in other cases of property … the same rules of evidence prevailed as in other cases relative to the right of property. … If, then, the same law exists in regard to property in slaves as in other things; and if documentary evidence, from the highest authority of the country where the property belonged, accompanied with possession, is produced; it follows that the title to the ownership of this property is as complete as is required by law."

After speaking for about two hours, Gilpin finished his argument and sat down.

Gilpin

While Adams was obviously the most well-known member of the Africans' team, he did not feel sufficiently prepared enough to argue the case when opening day rolled around, so he allowed Roger Sherman Baldwin, who had been the Africans' lawyer for longer, to take the lead.

Baldwin

After a summary of the events up until the time of the Supreme Court appeal, Baldwin began to list the reasons why the Court should indeed uphold the decisions handed down by the lower courts. In a politically astute move, he began by addressing the problem of Van Buren's interference in the case, an issue that many on both sides of the case agreed was wrong:

> "The Counsel for the Africans move the Court to dismiss this appeal, on the ground that the Executive Government of the United States had no right to become a party to the proceedings against them as property in the District Court, or to appeal from its decree.
>
> 1st. It was an unauthorized interference of the Executive with the appropriate duties of the Judiciary. ... And, it was long since remarked by an eminent jurist, that when either branch of the government usurps that part of the sovereignty which the constitution assigns to the other branch, liberty ends, and tyranny begins. The constitution designates the portion of sovereignty to be exercised by the judicial department, and among other attributes devolves upon it the cognizance of 'all cases in law or equity arising under the constitution, the laws of the United States, and treaties made or which shall be made under their authority' and 'all cases of admiralty and maritime jurisdiction and renders it sovereign, as to determinations

upon property, whenever that property is within its reach.'"

After elaborating on that argument for a while, Baldwin went on to his next point, which was that the United States had no right or obligation to protect the rights of slave ownership for people in other countries. Again, this was an excellent argument that many on both sides of the slavery issue could agree on. He explained:

> "2d. But if the Government of the United States could appear in any case as the representative of foreigners claiming property in the Court of Admiralty, it has no right to appear in their behalf to aid them in the recovery of fugitive slaves, even when domiciled in the country from which they escaped: much less the recent victims of the African slave trade, who have sought asylum in one of the free States of the Union.... The American people have never imposed it as a duty on the Government of the United States to become actors in an attempt to reduce to slavery men found in a state of freedom, by giving extra-territorial force to a foreign slave law. Such a duty would not only be repugnant to the feelings of a large portion of the citizens of the United States, but it would be wholly inconsistent with the fundamental principles of our Government, and the purposes for which it was established, as well as with its policy in prohibiting the slave trade and giving freedom to its victims."

Next, Baldwin addressed the importance of the case he was arguing. He knew that there was much more in question, and at stake, than simply the interests of those he represented. Indeed, there were many who were trying to cast the proceedings as a trial about America's "peculiar institution" – slavery – itself. The problem was that such arguments could either support or hurt Baldwin's case, and he wanted to try to make sure that it was the former rather than the latter:

> "This case is not only one of deep interest in itself as affecting the destiny of the unfortunate Africans whom I represent, but it involves considerations deeply affecting our national character in the eyes of the whole civilized world, as well as questions of power on the part of the government of the United States, which are regarded with anxiety and alarm by a large portion of our citizens. It presents, for the first time, the question whether that government, which was established for the promotion of justice, which was founded on the great principles of the Revolution, as proclaimed in the Declaration of Independence, can, consistently with the genius of our institutions, become a party to proceedings for the enslavement of human beings cast upon our shores, and found in the condition of freemen within the territorial limits of a FREE AND SOVEREIGN STATE. In the remarks I shall have occasion to make, it will be my design to appeal to no sectional prejudices, and to assume no positions in which I shall not hope to be sustained by intelligent minds from the South as well as from the North. Although I am in favor of the

broadest liberty of inquiry and discussion, — happily secured by our Constitution to every citizen, subject only to his individual responsibility to the laws for its abuse, — I have ever been of the opinion that the exercise of that liberty by citizens of one State in regard to the institutions of another should always be guided by discretion, and tempered with kindness."

After making his arguments about the rights of slaves within the United States in general, Baldwin next turned his attention to the specific question before the court, and he gave a specific and passionate answer: "We deny that Ruiz and Montes, Spanish subjects, had a right to call on any officer or Court of the United States to use the force of the government, or the process of the law for the purpose of again enslaving those who have thus escaped from foreign slavery, and sought an asylum here. We deny that the seizure of these persons by Lieutenant Gedney for such a purpose was a legal or justifiable act. How would it be -- independently of the treaty between the United States and Spain -- upon the principles of our government, of the common law, or of the law of nations? … Is there any principle of international law, or law of comity which requires it? Are our Courts bound, and if not, are they at liberty, to give effect here to the slave trade laws of a foreign nation; to laws affecting strangers, never domiciled there, when, to give them such effect would be to violate the natural rights of men? These questions are answered in the negative by all the most approved writers on the laws of nations."

Baldwin next went on to discuss the matter of whether or not the Africans were indeed legal slaves. Rather than get bogged down in the quagmire of the honesty of the Queen of Spain, he chose to take the high ground and focus on the actions of his own country's leadership: "But it is claimed that if these Africans, though "recently imported into Cuba," were by the laws of Spain the property of Ruiz and Montes, the government of the United States is bound by the treaty to restore them; and that, therefore, the intervention of the executive in these proceedings is proper for that purpose. It has already, it is believed, been shown that even if the case were within the treaty, the intervention of the executive as a party before the judicial tribunals was unnecessary and improper, since the treaty provides for its own execution by the Courts, on the application of the parties in interest."

Responding to Gilpin's claim that the Africans were indeed merchandise, Baldwin made an effective case that anyone who had been kidnapped illegally and then fought to obtain his own freedom could not be a slave but must indeed be a free man with the same rights as any other man who was free. He was particularly interested in the fact that the slaves obtained their freedom in international waters and thus had to be free at the time they arrived in the United States:

> "To render this clause of the treaty applicable to the case under consideration, it must be assumed that under the term 'merchandise' the contracting parties intended to include slaves…. … It is believed that such a construction of the words of the

treaty is not in accordance with the rules of interpretation which ought to govern our Courts; and that when there is no special reference to human beings as property, who are not acknowledged as such by the law of comity of nations generally, but only by the municipal laws of the particular nations which tolerate slavery, it cannot be presumed that the contracting parties intended to include them under the general term 'merchandise.' … But they were not pirates…. That object was … deliverance … from unlawful bondage. They owed no allegiance to Spain. They were on board of the *Amistad* by constraint. Their object was to free themselves from the fetters that bound them, in order that they might return to their kindred and their home. In so doing they were guilty of no crime, for which they could be held responsible as pirates."

Of course, there was still the matter of the treaty with Spain and what Americans owed their allies, as well as anyone who might have happened upon American shores. Again, the point hinged on whether or not the Africans were free when they arrived in America, and Baldwin maintained that they were: "If, indeed, the vessel in which they sailed had been driven upon our coast by stress of weather or other unavoidable cause, and they had arrived here in the actual possession of their alleged owners, and had been slaves by the law of the country from which they sailed, and where they were domiciled, it would have been a very different question…. But in this case there has been no possession of these Africans by their claimants within our jurisdiction, of which they have been deprived, by the act of our government or its officers; and neither by the law of comity, or by force of the treaty, are the officers or Courts of the United States required, or by the principles of our government permitted to become actors in reducing them to slavery."

The next day, on February 24, John Quincy Adams rose to speak. Utilizing both the gift of speaking he inherited from his father and the classical education given to him by his mother, Quincy Adams immediately launched into an incredibly eloquent argument:

> "[I]n a consideration of this case, I derive, in the distress I feel both for myself and my clients, consolation from two sources—first, that the rights of my clients to their lives and liberties have already been defended by my learned friend and colleague in so able and complete a manner as leaves me scarcely anything to say … and secondly, … from the thought that this Court is a Court of JUSTICE. And in saying so very trivial a thing I should not on any other occasion, perhaps, be warranted in asking the Court to consider what justice is. Justice, as defined in the Institutes of Justinian, nearly 2000 years ago, and as it felt and understood by all who understand human relations and human rights, is … 'The constant and perpetual will to secure to everyone HIS OWN right.' And in a Court of Justice, where there are two parties present, justice demands that the rights of each party should be allowed to himself, as well as that each party has a right, to be secured

and protected by the Court. This observation is important, because I appear here on the behalf of thirty-six individuals, the life and liberty of every one of whom depend on the decision of this Court."

Next, Quincy Adams addressed from his perspective the issue concerning Van Buren's interference in the case. Like Baldwin, he felt that the president was sticking his nose in where it did not belong. However, he must have been haunted somewhere in the back of his mind with similar accusations made against himself and even his beloved father in the past. While these memories did not stop him from doing his duty, it does seem to have made it particularly distasteful for him, as he mentioned: "When I say I derive consolation from the consideration that I stand before a Court of Justice, I am obliged to take this ground, because, as I shall -show, another Department of the Government of the United States has taken, with reference to this case, the ground of utter injustice, and these individuals for whom I appear, stand before this Court, awaiting their fate from its decision, under the array of the whole Executive power of this nation against them, in addition to that of a foreign nation. And here arises a consideration, the most painful of all others; in considering the duty I have to discharge, in which, in supporting the action to dismiss the appeal, I shall be obliged not only to investigate and submit to the censure of this Court, the form and manner of the proceedings of the Executive in this case, but the validity, and the motive of the reasons assigned for its interference in this unusual manner in a suit between parties for their individual rights."

Quincy Adams was only too aware that those to whom he was speaking would also be confused and perhaps even offended by his willingness to take on a fellow president. In fact, there no doubt were many who could not resist pointing out that Quincy Adams had something of an axe to grind with Van Buren since the latter had been part of the ticket that had denied him a second term in office. Not one to shy away from controversy, Quincy Adams addressed these silent concerns head on, saying, "It is, therefore, peculiarly painful to me, under present circumstances, to be under the necessity of arraigning before this Court and before the civilized world, the course of the existing Administration in this case. But I must do it. That Government is still in power, and thus, subject to the control of the Court, the lives and liberties of all my clients are in its hands. And if I should pass over the course it has pursued, those who have not kind an opportunity to examine the case and perhaps the Court itself, might decide that nothing improper had been done, and that the parties I represent had not been wronged by the course pursued by the Executive. … The charge I make against the present Executive administration is that in all their proceedings relating to these unfortunate men, instead of that Justice, which they were bound not less than this honorable Court itself to observe, they have substituted Sympathy! —sympathy with one of the parties in this conflict of justice, and antipathy to the other. Sympathy with the white, antipathy to the black…"

In addition to the obvious racism which he knew shaped the Justices' views of the case, Quincy Adams also enumerated the wrongs that had been done to the Africans from the very beginning of their encounters with the people of America, and how such wrongs combined to create a situation in which the only real way justice could be served would be by upholding the lower courts' decisions: "The whole of my argument to show that the appeal should be dismissed, is founded on an averment that the proceedings on the part of the United States are all wrongful from the beginning. The first act, of seizing the vessel, and these men, by an officer of the navy, was a wrong. The forcible arrest of these men, or a part of them, on the soil of New York, was a wrong. After the vessel was brought into the jurisdiction of the District Court of Connecticut, the men were first seized and imprisoned under a criminal process for murder and piracy on the high seas. Then they were libeled by Lieut. Gedney, as property, and salvage claimed on them, and under that process were taken into the Custody of the marshal as property. Then they were claimed by Ruiz and Montes and again taken into custody by the court."

The longer he spoke, the more passionate Quincy Adams became about his subject. He took on the very character of the Spanish monarchy and his own Secretary of State, John Forsyth, while citing the work of popular satirist Jonathan Swift to make his point: "I know not how, in decent language, to speak of this assertion of the Secretary, that the minister of Her Catholic Majesty had claimed the Africans 'as Spanish property.' In *Gulliver's Travels*, he is represented as traveling among a nation of beings, who were very rational in many things although they were not exactly human, and they had a very cool way of using language in reference to deeds that are not laudable. When they wished to characterize a declaration as absolutely contrary to truth, they say the man has 'said the thing that is not.' It is not possible for me to express the truth respecting this averment of the Secretary of State, but by declaring that he 'has said the thing that is not.' This I shall endeavor to prove by allowing what the demand of the Spanish minister was, and that it was a totally different thing from that which was represented."

Referring to letters that passed between Forsyth (writing on behalf of the president) and members of the Court, Quincy Adams pointed out the inconsistencies of both the language and the requests. His arguments came to a grand climax when he stated, "Now, how are all these demands to be put together? First, he demands that the United States shall keep them safely, and send them to Cuba, all in a lump, the children as well as Cinqué and Grabbo. Next, he denies the power of our courts to take any cognizance of the case. And finally, that the owners of the slaves shall be indemnified for any injury they may sustain in their property. We see in the whole of this transaction, a confusion of ideas and a contradiction of positions from confounding together the two capacities in which these people are attempted to be held. One moment they are viewed as merchandise, and the next as persons. The Spanish minister, the Secretary of State, and everyone who has had anything to do with the case, all have run into these absurdities. These demands are utterly inconsistent. First, they are demanded as persons, as the subjects of Spain, to be delivered up as criminals, to be tried for their lives, and liable to be executed on the gibbet. Then they are demanded as chattels, the same as so many bags of coffee, or bales of cotton, belonging to owners, who have a right to be indemnified for any injury to their property."

Since the Spanish government's arguments were based on treaties they held with the United States, Quincy Adams next turned his attention to the pertinent portions of those treaties for the Court. Having spent most of his time thus far speaking in terms of generalities and legal principles, he turned his attention to some hypothetical but nonetheless practical applications of the principles to help the Justices see whether or not the principles could be applied in the real life setting they were facing. He also drew particular attention to the fact that the slave trade was not only illegal in the United States but was also considered piracy, a capital offence: "But the article says the same assistance shall be afforded that our own citizens would be entitled to receive in like circumstances. Let us apply the rule. Suppose the *Amistad* had been a vessel of the United States, owned and manned by citizens of the United States, and in like circumstances. Say it was a Baltimore clipper, fitted for the African slave trade, and having performed a voyage, had come back to our shores, directly or indirectly, with fifty-four African victims on board, and was thus brought into port—what would be the assistance guaranteed by our laws to American citizens, in such circumstances? The captain would be seized, tried as a pirate, and hung! And every person concerned, either as owners or on board the ship, would be severely punished. The law makes it a capital offense for the captain, and no appeal to this Court would save him from the gibbet. Is that the assistance which the Spanish minister invokes for Ruiz and Montes? That is what our laws would secure to our own citizens in like circumstances. And perhaps it would be a reward nearer their merits than the restoration of these poor Negroes to them, or enabling them to complete their voyage."

Having arrived at the heart of the matter, Quincy Adams was now ready to bring his argument home. He again addressed the issue of whether the Africans were merchandise or crew and, bringing to bear the acerbic wit that made his father famous, showed the Court just how ridiculous his opponent's arguments were: "But my clients are claimed under the treaty as merchandise, rescued from pirates and robbers. Who were the merchandise, and who were the robbers? According to the construction of the Spanish minister, the merchandise were the robbers, and the robbers were the merchandise. The merchandise was rescued out of its own hands, and the robbers were rescued out of the hands of the robbers. Is this the meaning of the treaty? Will this Court adopt a rule of construction in regard to solemn treaties that will sanction such conclusions? There is a rule in Vattel that no construction shall be allowed to a treaty which makes it absurd. Is anything more absurd than to say these forty Africans are robbers, out of whose hands they have themselves been rescued? Can a greater absurdity be imagined in construction than this, which applies the double character of robbers and of merchandise to human beings?"

Quincy Adams spent much of the rest of his time speaking out against the bad behavior of the Secretary of State as it related to the matter, but during his long first day of speaking, he could not help but notice that one among his audience appeared to be ill. Indeed, the following morning, on February 25, Justice Philip Barbour died suddenly.

Justice Barbour

The court was forced to recess in respect and did not reconvene until March 1, at which point Quincy Adams reopened his arguments against the interference of the executive branch and the unlawful influence he felt it was trying to exert on the proceedings. After a brief mention of the loss of Justice Barbour, he launched his attack:

> "I said that my confidence in a favorable result to this trial rested mainly on the ground that I was now speaking before a Court of JUSTICE. And in moving the dismissal of the appeal taken on behalf of the United States, it became my duty, and was my object to show, by an investigation of all the correspondence of the Executive in regard to the case that JUSTICE had not been the motive of its proceedings, but that they had been prompted by sympathy with one of the two parties and against the other. In support of this, I must scrutinize, with the utmost severity every part of the proceedings of the Executive Government. ... I feel no unkind sentiments towards any of these gentlemen. With all of them, I am, in the private relations of life, on terms of intercourse, of the most friendly character. As to our political differences, let them pass for what they are worth, here they are nothing. ... I have been of the opinion that the case of my clients was so clear, so just, so righteous, that the Executive would do well to cease its prosecution, and leave the matter as it was decided by the District Court, and allow the appeal to be dismissed. But I did not succeed, and now I cannot do justice to my clients, whose lives and liberties depend on the decision of this Court—however painful it may be, to myself or others."

Quincy Adams then proceeded to a detailed examination of the four demands made by the Secretary of State to the Court on behalf of the Spanish government. After explaining in great detail why each request was wrongfully made, or at the very least did not deserve to be heard, he concluded his arguments with a lengthy review of the case of the *Antelope*. After hearing that case in 1821, the Supreme Court returned almost 100 slaves captured off the coast of Florida to Africa. After his review of that case, Adams argued that "the opinion of the Supreme Court, as declared by the Chief Justice, in the case of the Antelope, was a fact, an authority in point, against the surrender of the *Amistad*, and in favor of the liberation of the Africans taken in her, even if they had been, when taken, in the condition of slaves."

Following his review of the *Antelope*, Quincy Adams briefly mentioned to the Court that he had not presented a case before it since 1809, more than 30 years earlier, and that he had only returned on this one occasion because of the gravity of the matter. He concluded with words that reminded the Justices of the Court's illustrious past and their obligation to its future:

> "As I cast my eyes along those seats of honor and of public trust, now occupied by you, they seek in vain for one of those honored and honorable persons whose indulgence listened then to my voice. Marshall—Cushing—Chase—Washington—Johnson—Livingston— Todd—Where are they? ... Gone! Gone! All gone! — Gone from the services which, in their day and generation, they faithfully rendered to their country. From the excellent characters which they sustained in life, so far as I have had the means of knowing, I humbly hope, and fondly trust, that they have gone to receive the rewards of blessedness on high. In taking, then, my final leave of this Bar, and of this Honorable Court, I can only ejaculate a fervent petition to Heaven, that every member of it may go to his final account with as little of earthly frailty to answer for as those illustrious dead, and that you may, every one, after the close of a long and virtuous career in this world, be received at the portals of the next with the approving sentence—'Well done, good and faithful servant; enter thou into the joy of thy Lord.'"

Gilpin rose again on March 2, 1941 to offer a rebuttal to the arguments made by Baldwin and Quincy Adams, and after he spoke for nearly three hours, the Court recessed and retired to deliberate.

John Quincy Adams in 1843

Chapter 6: The Ruling

A page from the text of the Supreme Court decision

Justice Story

"It is also a most important consideration, in the present case, which ought not to be lost sight of, that, supposing these African negroes not to be slaves, but kidnapped, and free negroes, the treaty with Spain cannot be obligatory upon them; and the United States are bound to respect their rights as much as those of Spanish subjects." – The majority opinion of the Supreme Court in *United States v. Libellants and Claimants of the Schooner Amistad*

A week after the oral arguments ended, on March 9, Justice Joseph Story announced the Court's decision. In a 7-1 vote, the remaining Justices ruled that the Africans aboard the *Amistad* had never been the legal property of anyone:

> "[I]t is clear, in our opinion, that neither of the other essential facts and requisites has been established in proof; and the onus probandi of both lies upon the claimants

to give rise to the causes foederis. It is plain beyond controversy, if we examine the evidence, that these Negroes never were the lawful slaves of Ruiz or Montes, or of any other Spanish subjects. They are natives of Africa, and were kidnapped there, and were unlawfully transported to Cuba, in violation of the laws and treaties of Spain, and the most solemn edicts and declarations of that government. By those laws, and treaties, and edicts, the African slave trade is utterly abolished; the dealing in that trade is deemed a heinous crime; and the Negroes thereby introduced into the dominions of Spain, are declared to be free. Ruiz and Montes are proved to have made the pretended purchase of these Negroes, with a full knowledge of all the circumstances. And so cogent and irresistible is the evidence in this respect, that the District Attorney has admitted in open Court, upon the record, that these Negroes were native Africans, and recently imported into Cuba, as alleged in their answers to the libels in the case. The supposed proprietary interest of Ruiz and Montes, is completely displaced, if we are at liberty to look at the evidence of the admissions of the District Attorney."

Story further added that, in the eyes of the Court, the Africans also were guilty of no crime but instead had been "unlawfully kidnapped, and forcibly and wrongfully carried on board a certain vessel." Thus, there was no legal reason for the United States to hold them to face charges in America or return them to Spain to be tried: "If, then, these Negroes are not slaves, but are kidnapped Africans, who, by the laws of Spain itself, are entitled to their freedom, and were kidnapped and illegally carried to Cuba, and illegally detained and restrained on board of the *Amistad*; there is no pretense to say, that they are pirates or robbers. We may lament the dreadful acts, by which they asserted their liberty, and took possession of the *Amistad*, and endeavored to regain their native country; but they cannot be deemed pirates or robbers in the sense of the law of nations, or the treaty with Spain, or the laws of Spain itself; at least so far as those laws have been brought to our knowledge."

Perhaps just as importantly, the Court ruled that there was no obligation on the part of the President of the United States, or any other member of the government, to return the Africans to their homeland. Instead, they were free men and could decide for themselves where they wanted to live: "When the *Amistad* arrived she was in possession of the Negroes, asserting their freedom; and in no sense could they possibly intend to import themselves here, as slaves, or for sale as slaves. In this view of the matter, that part of the decree of the District Court is unmaintainable, and must be reversed. ... Upon the whole, our opinion is, that the decree of the Circuit Court, affirming that of the District Court, ought to be affirmed, except so far as it directs the Negroes to be delivered to the President, to be transported to Africa, in pursuance of the act of the 3d of March, 1819; and, as to this, it ought to be reversed: and that the said Negroes be declared to be free, and be dismissed from the custody of the Court, and go without delay."

Needless to say, the ruling was met with great rejoicing among the Africans and those who had so dutifully fought for their rights. As soon as they were freed from their jail cells, the abolitionists arranged for the 39 Africans who had survived the long voyage, mutiny, and imprisonment to stay in nearby Farmington, Connecticut, where they could decide what they wanted to do. While they lived in Farmington, the Africans continued to receive instruction in Christianity and the Friends Committee continued to raise money to finance a return trip to Africa for those who wished to return. Several of the abolitionists even offered to accompany the Africans to their homes and remain there as missionaries, which led to the establishment of the American Missionary Association. In turn, the American Missionary Association ultimately founded Howard University, one of the country's foremost traditionally black colleges.

In November 1841, the Africans and their missionary sponsors returned to Sierra Leone, and once there, they were reunited with their families and assisted in establishing the first of many Christian missions on the continent. However, before they left, some of the Africans wrote a letter to the one they most credited with their freedom. In May 1841, John Quincy Adams received the following, along with a most fitting gift: "We thank you very much because you make us free and because you love all Mendi people. They give you money for Mendi people and you say you will not take it, because you love Mendi people. ... Wicked people want to make us slaves but the great God who has made all things raise up friends for Mendi people he give us Mr. Adams that he may make me free and all Mendi people free. ... [W]e write this to you because you plead with the Great Court to make us free and now we are free and joyful we thank the Great God. I hope God will bless you dear friend. Mendi people will remember you when we go to our own country and we will tell all our friends about you and we will say to them Mr. Adams is a great man and he plead for us and how very glad we be and our friends will love you very much because you was a very good man and oh how joyful we shall be. ... Dear Friend I called you my Father because you set us free. Mendi people thank you very much and we will pray for you every day and night that God will keep you from danger. Dear Sir who make you to become great President over America people God – God make everything. He make men to do good and love one another. ... Mr Adams We write our names for you in this Bible that you may remember Mendi people. ... Kali, Cinqui, Cici, Kinna, Faliama, Barma, Tagino, Batu."

A memorial commemorating the *Amistad* located at Montauk Point State Park on Long Island

Bibliography

Jackson, Donald Dale (1997). "Mutiny on the Amistad". Smithsonian 28

Jones, Howard (1987). *Mutiny on the Amistad: The Saga of a Slave Revolt and Its Impact on American Abolition, Law, and Diplomacy*. New York: Oxford University Press.

Osagie, Iyunolu Folayan (2000). *The Amistad Revolt: Memory, Slavery, and the Politics of Identity in the United States and Sierra Leone*. Athens: University of Georgia Press.

Owens, William A. (1997). Black Mutiny: The Revolt on the Schooner Amistad,

Pesci, David (1997) Amistad, Da Capo Press

Rediker, Marcus. (2012). *The Amistad Rebellion: An Atlantic Odyssey of Slavery and Freedom*. New York: Viking.

Zeuske, Michael (2014). "Rethinking the Case of the Schooner Amistad: Contraband and Complicity after 1808/1820". Slavery & Abolition 35